WOMEN IN TIME AND SPACE

ANSWERING THE CALL OF
PURPOSE WHEN WE HAVE
LESS TIME THAN EVER

Jessica Mehring

WOMEN IN TIME AND SPACE

ANSWERING THE CALL OF
PURPOSE WHEN WE HAVE
LESS TIME THAN EVER

Jessica Mehring

Five Bears Press
Colorado Springs, CO

Copyright © 2020 by Jessica Mehring

Cover art: Josiah Weiss

All rights reserved. No part of this publication may be reproduced, distributed or transmitted in any form or by any means, including photocopying, recording, or other electronic or mechanical methods, without the prior written permission of the publisher, except in the case of brief quotations embodied in critical reviews and certain other noncommercial uses permitted by copyright law. For permission requests, write to the publisher, addressed "Attention: Permissions Coordinator," at the address below.

Five Bears Press
6510-A South Academy Blvd. #121
Colorado Springs, CO 80906

Ordering Information:
Quantity sales. Special discounts are available on quantity purchases by corporations, associations, and others. For details, contact the "Special Sales Department" at the address above.

Women in Time and Space / Jessica Mehring. — 1st ed.
ISBN 978-1-7354013-0-0

CONTENTS

Introduction: Your Voice Matters, No Matter How You Choose to Express It...................... 1

    Chapter 1: Don't Let Your Dreams Die Trapped Inside You 7

Today in Time 11

    Chapter 2: The Power You Hold 12

    Chapter 3: The Stark Truth of Our Relational Nature 17

    Chapter 4: State of Tension.....................22

Back in Time...29

    Chapter 5: Models of Success..................30

    Chapter 6: Carrying the Relics of Those Who Died in Battle 38

Lost and Found 67

    Chapter 7: My Story.................................68

    Chapter 8: The Time I Lost and the Time I Gained..70

    Chapter 9: When Time Is Paused............96

Conclusion: Mustangs in a World of Pretty Ponies 98

Works Cited... 102

Acknowledgements 103

About the Author 104

Dedicated to the women who went before, who carved a path for me — and to Jeremy, who never stopped believing I could carve a path for our daughters.

Introduction

Your Voice Matters, No Matter How You Choose to Express It

P urpose. Passion. These are scary words. They can trigger feelings of inadequacy and confusion — *Who am I to want this? What IS my purpose or passion?*

Or they can trigger feelings of angst — *I'm never going to have time to pursue that ... I can't make enough money doing that to dedicate my time to it ...*

Scary as those words are, though, I believe they've been put on our hearts for a reason.

We are here for a purpose.

Each and every one of us is here to do *a work in the world.*

"A work in the world" is not the work you do to make a living (at least for most of us). Your work in the world is your calling, the way you're changing people or this planet during your time here, the mark you're meant to leave, the message you're meant to convey, the beauty you were put here to bring to fruition.

As a Christian, I believe that God planted this seed in our spirits when He created us. If you follow a different spiritual path, by all means, think of God in the way that resonates so you can hear this very important message:

You have a purpose here, and no matter how insignificant you might think that it is, it is *powerful* and it is *needed* —

and it's time to stop putting it on the back burner.

We women have been quiet too long. Our voices have been dampened by culture and systems and beliefs — but don't let anyone ever convince you they were dampened by *biology*. There is nothing in the biology of the female body that makes our work in this world any less important, or that demands we must shut up and maintain the status quo.

When women raise their voices, mountains get up and move.

Your voice and how you choose to express it through your work in the world *matters*.

And no, even with all our progress, it's still not easy to answer the call of our purpose and do our work in the world. It's still a challenge, and it's still not always accepted by the people around us. But we must find a way through.

It's time to demand more than a room of our own. It's time to demand *time* of our own.

It's not easy — but it's necessary. This world is crying out for it just as our spirits are crying out for it. Women are burning out, succumbing to depression, giving up — and the world is suffering for it. Our children see adulthood as a flame extinguished. Our marriages stand on a shaky foundation of shared duties, if they stand at all. Our jobs are just thieves of time and energy. *We need more than this.*

We were put here for more than this.

Yes, there are seasons when our voices are quieter — especially in seasons when we're deeply focused on caring for others who can't care for themselves. Even in seasons of quiet, though, we must ensure that our voices are never *muted*. We are here to do a work in the world. We are here to be heard. God doesn't make mistakes — He planted a seed in your heart for a reason.

This is what I want you to take away from this tiny book. You were put here for a purpose — no matter how small or frivolous you might feel your calling to be. Each one of us plays a part in making this world a better place, whether it's through writing or art or community engagement or politics or *whatever*. That purpose, that calling, that's your work in the world, and it deserves your time and attention. Or rather, *you* deserve to give it time and attention. Because it's when we're doing our work in the world that we are in alignment with not just ourselves, but our Creator as well.

There's a reason you are called to certain activities, whatever they may be. God has put this seed in you expecting it to grow into a mighty oak. For some, the seed is clearly planted for the purpose of helping others (individuals and/or communities). For others, the seed was planted to help the earth, or the collective spirit. Still other seeds were planted to bring beauty into the world. Some seeds may seem purely selfish at first, but as they take root and grow, they change you — and your renewed spirit has a positive ripple effect in the world.

We're already giving so much of ourselves to others every single day — our partners, our children, our friends, family members, bosses, colleagues. At the end of the day, our calling can feel like another relationship to manage. By the end of this book, I hope it feels more like a well-deserved reward.

To make this shift, nurture the seed of our purpose, and make a difference in this world, we must reclaim time for ourselves. It's not easy — women have come so far, but taking the time we need for ourselves is still not easy. In fact, I might argue it's harder than ever.

I have taken great inspiration from studying women in history who made a mark on this world. In this book, we're going to look to a few of the women who paved the path for us so that today we can more confidently answer the calling that God put on our hearts. I'm also going to share some of my own story of finding time to do my work in this world in the hopes that something in my experience will help you or inspire you.

CHAPTER 1

Don't Let Your Dreams Die Trapped Inside You

For too many years, I denied my calling to write books. I had written a few books, but had never really made a career of it because — I admit it — I had money goggles on. I thought I couldn't make enough money writing books. I fell into copywriting fresh out of college, and that seemed like a more viable career path, so that's the direction I went. I knew I would make money as a copywriter, and that skillset would always be in demand.

I got really, really good at it. I specialized in writing marketing content (white papers, blog posts, e-books, email series, etc.) for technology companies, I figured out a process that worked well to help those companies reach their marketing goals, and my reputation grew quickly.

After a while I convinced myself it was enough. I told myself I was blessed to be able to write for a living, even if it was "writing to order" in some ways.

Over the years, I added to the story I was telling myself. I told myself I wasn't capable of writing fiction anymore. I'd lost my imagination. I told myself that writing nonfiction books was a waste of time. I didn't have anything valuable to teach, and I didn't have a big enough platform for a publisher to want to work with me.

Eventually I told myself I was too old to write books. The dream had passed me by.

Then my youngest brother died.

After college, he struggled to start his life ... and he never really did start his life before he died at age 36. When he died, all his dreams, and all my parents' dreams for him, died too. His death was sudden and unexpected, and it shook me to my core.

Losing my brother broke the spell I had inadvertently placed over my writing. It wasn't conscious, really — all signs just began to point to me writing again. Writing was the seed God planted in me, the work I was meant to do in the world. I didn't want to die with this seed unnurtured.

I didn't know how this would play out. But it didn't matter anymore. All that mattered was that I had to do the work that I was born to do. The outcome wasn't my responsibility — only the work.

It was this realization, in part, that spurred me to make more time for writing. It was also what made me see the bind I was in. My life revolved around caring for others — my family, my clients — and I was cramming time for writing into the nooks and crannies. It's not a new story. It's the same bind many women find themselves in today. We've not only succumbed to the systems we were born into, we've bound ourselves to the systems, too.

Unbinding myself and prioritizing time for my work in the world was an arduous process. It also taught me a lot about myself and the world around me. While I'm far from done with this journey, I believe that what I've learned so far may be enough to shift someone's perspective and move them more fully into their purpose. And if I can help just one woman to unbind herself and take time to do her unique work in the world, the time I put into writing this tiny book will be worth it.

Today in Time

CHAPTER 2

The Power You Hold

Not long ago, I was rereading a book from one of my college courses. The book revolved around humanist "learned women" (women who studied and wrote) in Renaissance Italy, and featured many of their letters in the text.

To me, a modern woman, the letters were both beautiful and cringeworthy. They were florid and rich, and yet full of exaggerated humility and blatant flattery. Here are some examples:

I, of inferior sex, have set out to write to you, most glorious hero ...

Aware of the weakness of my sex and the paucity of my talent, blushing, I decided to honor and obey him

...

I fear that your lofty opinion of me may spring from some other source than a carefully balanced judgment.

There was a purpose behind this deferential language, though. Showing humility to the point of expressing deep inferiority was part of the etiquette of the time, but especially for women it was important to preface their statements properly in order to *earn the right* to be heard by men.

Today we might call that "qualifying language." As in, adding qualifiers around statements to soften them or hedge them.

Here's the thing: We women still use qualifiers in our language all too often.

The verbiage has changed — instead of "I, of inferior sex" we say "This is just a thought, but … " "Well, I'm not expert, but … " "It seems that maybe … " — but the hedging quality is the same. It serves to minimize the impact of our words, keep the boat from rocking, and *make us small*.

What shocked me was that I started finding a lot of this qualifying language when women were sharing critical information during the recent major social upheaval here in the U.S. As women shared resources around protests and movements, and tried to elevate others' voices by sharing social media content, they were starting their posts with language like "I'm sure I'm doing this wrong, but ... "

STILL. We are *still* diminishing ourselves. It's not enough that we've been diminished throughout history, we're continuing to do it to ourselves.

It broke my heart to read those messages. I wanted to shout at them: *You're saying something important! Stop killing your message!*

Words have power. The power to hurt, to heal, and to change the world. The words we choose to use have outsized impact on the results we're seeking. Beyond the spiritual implication of watching what we say, we must also be conscious of how our words are wiring our own brains, and how they're being taken and used by other people.

For example, the difference between "I don't have time" and "I'm spending my time on other things right now" is the difference between drought and a dry patch. A drought is devastating and enduring. A dry patch is time between rain showers — short lived, with the promise of life.

You are here for a reason. You are here for a purpose. You have a calling. This world is hard on a woman — it's always been hard on us. We might be able to vote and own property today, but that doesn't make it any easier to find the space and time to do our work in the world.

The first thing I will ask you to do as you read this book is to watch your language. Where are you adding unnecessary qualifiers like *just*, *maybe*, *appears*, or *possibly*? How are you describing your struggle to find time and energy to do your work in the world? Are your statements fatalistic (e.g. *I'll never get around to this.*) or dismissive (e.g. *I'm not good enough at this anyway.*)?

If you're struggling to find the energy to paint, getting writer's block when you get five minutes of peace at your laptop, have a dream for a non-profit that you can't seem to find time to pursue — you're not broken. You're not weak. You're not failing. You're living in the 21st century, and by simply acknowledging that you want to nurture that seed of purpose inside you, you're carving a better path for future generations.

Be confident in how you're communicating about your work in this world. It matters.

CHAPTER 3

The Stark Truth of Our Relational Nature

One of the most destructive concepts, I believe, in the modern conversation about women as leaders, and women in the workplace especially, is that *women are more relational than men.*

What does that mean, exactly, that women are more relational than men? The *idea* is that women place more importance on relationship, and by extension, communication and collaboration. In reality, though, it often gets twisted to mean that we value relationship over anything else, including our own wellbeing.

Brigid Schulte drives this home in her brilliant and heartbreaking article for The Guardian, *A woman's greatest enemy? A lack of time to herself*: "One study of 32 families in Los Angeles found that the uninterrupted leisure time of most mothers lasted, on average, no more than 10 minutes at a stretch. ... But the women's time at work, too, was interrupted and fragmented, chopped up with more service work, mentoring and teaching. The men spent more of their work days in long stretches of uninterrupted time to think, research, write, create and publish to make their names, advance their careers and get their ideas out into the world."

When people say that women are *relational*, that's often code for *martyr*.

By default, we're culturally conditioned to take care of others first — and these days, we are conditioned to do it alone. Even if we have a partner or colleagues who are willing and able to offer support, we still more often care for others (our children, our partners, our aging parents, our team members) individually, not collaboratively. Our first and most important responsibilities are to others, and asking for help is a sign that you don't have it all together. The result is you're always putting everyone else first, and your own work in the world goes on the back burner.

I fell into this trap for too long. If I wasn't doing work that was resulting in money, I felt like I had better be taking care of the kids. I wouldn't do a thing other than work or parent without asking for permission from my husband, who was a stay-at-home dad, because only that permission would assuage the guilt of doing something that wasn't providing income for my family or directly taking care of them. And I rarely asked for this permission, because it felt like I was putting more of a burden on Jeremy, who was home with the kids all day while I worked.

The only real break I got from working or caring for others, then, was when my kids were asleep and Jeremy was downstairs watching a movie I didn't want to watch. Weekdays I worked; weekends I cared for the kids and gave Jeremy a break. There was little time for my own work — my writing, my art — and I was *exhausted* in the little time I had.

This isn't the freedom we were promised when our mothers told us we could have it all.

Modern life has just created new prisons.

David Whyte in his book, *The Three Marriages*, said that a woman risks more than any man will understand when she falls in love: She risks childbearing. She risks being fatally vulnerable to an insincere man. When a woman chooses to marry, and especially when she chooses to have a child, she risks literal death.

This may sound extreme, but our commitments to our loved ones *are* risks to our lives. This commitment to relationship, when unchecked, can kill our ability to do our work in the world and move into the purpose God has put us here for.

Modern culture would have you believe that you must be relational, above all — keep your relationships healthy and strong. This is your duty. (Note it's never the *man's* duty to maintain the relationship.)

We've come so far, but even today we kill ourselves in relationship. We're martyrs with no witnesses to spread the message — we accept the burdens of others in order to ease *their* burdens.

It's not okay. It's not healthy. Like putting the oxygen mask on yourself first, you can't be your best for others when you're not taking care of yourself.

A critical part of taking care of ourselves is carving out the time to do our own work in the world.

CHAPTER 4

State of Tension

We live in a constant state of tension — the tight rubber band stretched between work and home; self and others; the desire for stability and the need for freedom; the compromises we make and the rights we demand. We know that every rubber band eventually breaks when it's stretched tight enough long enough — so anxiety is a natural side effect of this tension.

No human mind can remain healthy and whole in a constant state of tension, waiting for the rubber band to snap ... because we know that's going to hurt. We're anticipating *pain*, not just the unraveling of the thing we've built.

What often starts to stretch us is the striving for balance. We want balance between work and home, duty and pleasure, time with family and time alone. We keep stretching those rubber bands from one end to the other, and society lauds us for it. When it inevitably snaps — when we realize that we're not balancing anything, but rather stretching too far — we experience emotional and psychic pain. Not just because we feel like we failed, but also because we want more for ourselves. The snap is a sharp reminder that we're human and we have human limitations.

The people who *don't* struggle as much with this tension (men, particularly), understand that to choose one thing means giving up another. They don't try to have it all. They choose the thing they want. They make it a choice. They see life as a meal, not a smorgasbord. They order off the menu of life instead of trying to stack multiple plates with food from the buffet.

To be fair to men, throughout history we women have eliminated choices for them, leaving them with a lean menu and lowering the decision overwhelm factor. Raising children was taken off their menu. So was taking care of the home. The emotional health of the marriage was not on the list, and planning for the future was a seasonal selection. Historically speaking, if women tried to put these things back on the menu for their male partners, those men would go to another restaurant and leave the woman with the bill.

Things are different in so many ways today, and we have put more items on the menu for men. Unfortunately, women's buffets have also gotten bigger, and we're still trying to stack our plates.

There's no easy answer to this. Massive societal and relational shifts don't happen overnight. We do need to realize, though, that we are living in a state of tension, trying to be so many things for so many people, and we need to separate our work in the world from this structure.

The alternative is that the seedling of purpose we are trying to nurture gets snapped when the rubber band breaks.

Protect the seedling.

The Choice Between Angst and Regret

Let me be clear: The state of tension is natural. Trying to strike balances in your life is natural (even if balance is actually impossible). Most of us don't have the option to unhook one side of the rubber band to release the strain.

Recognizing that we live in this tension, though, reveals the landscape we're navigating. It's like being lost in the woods, then pulling out a map and orienting yourself to a landmark. You're still in the woods, but now you have a good idea of how to get where you're going.

For the longest time, I refused to get out my map. Not only was I lost in the woods, I was sitting on a boulder pouting about it.

Virginia Woolf said that a woman needs a room of her own and money of her own in order to create. I had a room of my own. I had money of my own. And yet I was still unable to get any truly creative work done — writing fiction or otherwise. The experts all said "rise before your children in the morning and do your creative work then." I scoffed. I have always wanted to be a morning person — oh, I've tried *everything* to rise early — but I've always felt most creative at night. Even if I *could* manage to get up early, I wouldn't be able to write first thing. My brain needs input before it's ready to perform. (Which is why another popular piece of productivity advice doesn't work for me: That is, don't check email or watch the news first thing in the morning.) My body's rhythms were in direct contrast with what the experts said I had to do to be a successful writer.

I submitted to my age, believing there were things I could change at that point in life (late 30s at this point) and things I couldn't. I whined to Jeremy about having no energy to write. I envied the larks who rose early and beat the day to the punch.

The experts also say to ask for the help you need. I needed uninterrupted time to write, and I couldn't ask for it. Not because Jeremy wouldn't have given it to me, but because *I wanted time with my kids*. AND I wanted time with my husband. Those were important things too!

This was the conundrum I found myself in. I knew that life goes by quickly. I knew that my children would be grown and gone in the blink of an eye. I also knew that the longer I put off my writing, the less likely I was to actually do it.

Each minute as a choice. And each choice has a consequence.

The truth is, I was making things too black and white.

I saw parenthood as a choice between angst and regret.

The parents I knew who weren't around much when their kids were growing up (usually it was because they were pursuing a career) ended up regretting it. They felt like they had missed out, and what they were pursuing wasn't worth what they gave up for it.

The parents I knew who chose to focus on their families when their kids were growing up had no regrets. They could sleep well at night knowing they did the best they could for their families. But these parents were also wistful, full of stories about the things they used to do before they had kids ... things they put down and never picked up again. There was a feeling of gnawing angst in how they described their experiences.

If that is the choice, I thought, I'll take the angst now and avoid the regret later.

I was knowingly, purposefully choosing angst.

It turns out, there was a third option: reclaiming.

I will share my story with you in this book — and share how I reclaimed time to do my work in the world (how I'm *still* reclaiming it) — but not just yet. There are other women's stories I wish to tell first.

Back in Time

CHAPTER 5

Models of Success

My grandmother had seven children. Six girls and one very spoiled boy. She stayed at home with them while my grandfather built (and lost and rebuilt) his empire. She wasn't on her own with those seven kids, however — she had help in the form of hired housekeepers and nannies. And when my grandfather broke his back in a plane crash, she had nurses to help her care for him as well.

My mother had a different experience raising kids. She didn't have help. She took care of my brothers and I while my father went to work every day. Even if it was socially acceptable to hire help (which for a middle class family then, it really wasn't) they couldn't afford it. My mother couldn't afford to work for 10 years after I was born, either — not until my brothers and I were all in school full time. Daycare for three kids cost more than she could make at a job, even with her business degree from Berkeley.

My mom was part of the first generation that was expected to both take care of the children and house full-time *and* contribute financially to the household. And frankly, I don't know how she survived it.

My husband, Jeremy, has been a stay-at home dad since we had our first child back in 2010. With him taking point with the kids and house during the work week, I've been able to start and grow a profitable business that supports our family. Like my mother, I'm expected to contribute both financially and with childcare (outside of working hours, at least) — but unlike her, the responsibilities of children and house are not *all on me*.

And yet. *And yet*. I still felt stifled for many years. I still didn't have time to do all the things I wanted to do, because when I wasn't working, I was taking point with my kids so I could have time with them and so Jeremy could have a break. (Because I know if I were the at-home parent, I would need a break!)

So the roles my husband and I have aren't reversed in a straightforward way. Rather, they're reimagined.

This reimagining is a common thread among the women in history who have done great works in the world. After doing some research on historical female figures to explore in this book, I now wonder if they reimagined more than their own daily routines. I wonder if they reimagined the future for women everywhere.

On May 22, 2020, I did a Google search for "most prolific women in history," hoping to get a list of female creators who had produced a lot of work. The result was ... not what I expected. The Google algorithm's definition of "prolific" was apparently "had a lot of children."

Females and monogamous couples

No. of children	Mother/couple
69	Mrs. and Mr. Feodor Vassilyev (1st wife)
62	Mr. and Mrs. Gravata
57	Mrs. and Mr. Yakov Kirillov
53	Barbara and Adam Stratzmann

91 more rows

en.wikipedia.org › wiki › List_of_people_with_the_mo... ▼
◐ List of people with the most children - Wikipedia

When I think of "prolific women," I think of women who have *produced a quantity of great work*. By all means, children are a great work of their own — but producing children is different than producing novels or paintings or great societal change.

This Google search results page is an indication, to me, of how women have been viewed throughout history — as having the primary role of producing children. Even with all our progress, we can't shake that, it seems. Google's algorithm is based in part on what content people are engaging with when they search on keywords. So enough people have clicked on and spent time reading articles about human baby-making machines after searching on the term "most prolific women in history" to tell the algorithm that this is what people want to see when they search on this key phrase.

When I sat in the shock of these search results for a while, though, another thought occurred to me. Perhaps the women who went before us reimagined the world so well that they *changed the definition of "prolific."* The word comes from the Latin root *prolificus*, meaning "offspring," and yet we talk about prolific writers, prolific artists, even prolific speakers.

I have always loved to read books about mindset, productivity, creativity and habits — and I am a huge fan of authors who use historical figures to illustrate real-world applications of their concepts. Ryan Holiday and Robert Greene are two of my favorites. And yet, their work also devastates me.

Most of the historical figures they reference are men (with or without children), and any women they reference are typically wealthy and childless. In either case, these people would have had few (or no) responsibilities around caring for other human beings, and minimal responsibilities around caring for themselves. Someone else cooked the food, cleaned the house, mended the clothes, ran the errands — and in the case of the men, someone else cared for the children.

These models are IMPOSSIBLE for any mother — in any period of time — to follow. I was reading these books about people who have done amazing things in this world, yearning to do something amazing myself, feeling like if only I could follow these famous people's daily routines and adopt their habits, I could be a huge success too ...

And it was Winston Churchill that woke me up to reality.

In his book *Stillness Is the Key*, Ryan Holiday wrote about Winston Churchill's morning routine — which involved leisurely bathing, reading, and responding to mail — and how this routine helped Churchill stay focused on the important work he was doing in the world. What struck me when I was reading it was that *Churchill didn't see his wife until noon each day.* My immediate thought was, *My husband and kids would disown me if I didn't see them until noon every day.* ... and then that thought was quickly followed by *Wait a minute ... Churchill is a man. The majority of these examples of success I'm reading about are men, or wealthy women without kids ... they can get away with that kind of behavior! I can't! No mother can!*

Let's face it. Most productivity and habits books are written with men in mind. They tell you that successful people rise at 5 a.m., meditate for 20 minutes, then exercise, journal, and make a green smoothie. That sounds glorious — but when your kids start waking at 5:30 or 6 in the morning, it's impossible. The books tell you that successful people focus on activities that make a positive impact in the world. But when you're working full-time to put food on the table for a family of four, helping with homework between the end of your workday and the start of you cooking dinner each night, and then collapsing in bed a half hour after your kids do because you'll be up to start it all over again at 5:30 the next morning, "impact" is the least of your worries.

Most productivity and habits books are utopian. They paint a picture of a pretty little life where you're only responsible for yourself. The reality for most of us is that we have other people in our lives who need our time and attention — and every decision we make impacts them.

So are we victims of our womanhood, then? Are we doomed to cram our purpose-driven work into the nooks and crannies of an overstuffed life?

Far from it.

CHAPTER 6

Carrying the Relics of Those Who Died in Battle

Throughout time, in cultures all around the world, leaders in wartime did something that we might find creepy today. Marching onto the field of war, they carried relics — reminders of family members and countrymen who died in battle … and sometimes these reminders were *body parts.*

I suppose it makes a little more sense when you think about relics from a spiritual standpoint. Many religions honor the paraphernalia, bones, hair, etc. of dead saints and spiritual leaders. It's creepy when you really think about it, but really, it's not that far out there. Reminders of those who were courageous, whether spiritually or on the battlefield, can give us strength. They give our anxiety-filled minds something to focus on, at least.

When I think of the creative, world-changing women who have gone before me, I am stirred. I feel bolder, hungrier. These women were operating within constraints I couldn't even dream of, and they still did their work in the world. While the context of their lives doesn't always translate directly to the context of ours, there are elements (routines, habits, mindsets, activities) that we can pluck from their lives and plant in the gardens of our own.

In many ways, the physical manifestations of these women's callings — their books and paintings and poetry and speeches and the impact they made on the people they encountered — serve as relics to me. I carry them with me, sometimes literally in the form of books, but often just in my heart and spirit, and they remind me that nothing is impossible if I set my mind to it.

My hope is that you'll carry some of these stories with you, too. Let them be reminders that we are strong, innovative world-builders ... and our work in this world *matters.*

Virginia Woolf: Don't Let Others' Expectations Steal Your Voice

"Mom, that boy is NAKED!" my four-year old shouted as we drove down the hill past a shirtless teenage jogger.

"He's not naked, honey. He's just not wearing a shirt. Boys can do that. Girls can't." For it seems like the millionth time in the last year, I heard the words coming out of my mouth and cringed at their deeper meaning.

What I said was sexist on every level.

Black and white language is also the clearest way to explain almost anything to a young child.

I've always bristled at the implication that the rules of life should be different for a woman versus a man. I bristle, but I know how to navigate it — I've got more than 40 years of practice under my belt, now.

As a mother, though, bristling and navigating doesn't cut it. My daughters demand *explanations*. Why can a boy go shirtless and a girl can't? Why do women shave and men don't? Why doesn't Daddy wear makeup, and why do *you* wear it, Mama?

How do you answer those questions without revealing a deep and jagged line between society's differing expectations of men and women?

We may have more legal rights today than ever before. We may be able to work outside the home, keep the money we make, expect the police to help us if our partners raise their hands to us, have children outside of wedlock — or choose not to have children at all — but still, the expectations placed on us in society are radically different from those placed on men.

Virginia Woolf saw this and called it out. In *A Room of One's Own*, she called out the patriarchy ...

> *"The most transient visitor to this planet, I thought, who picked up this paper could not fail to be aware, even from this scattered testimony, that England is under the rule of a patriarchy."*

and questioned the anger many men of her time held toward women ...

> *"The indifference of the world which Keats and Flaubert and other men of genius have found so hard to bear was in her case not indifference but hostility."*

and she did it openly through her writing and speaking. I'll never forget the first time I read *A Room of One's Own*. I was in awe at how brazen she was in a time where women were still viciously punished for being brazen. I wondered how she got away with it, honestly.

Then I wondered why I didn't feel like *I* could get away with it a hundred years and so many more human rights later.

Born in England in 1882, Virginia Woolf grew up in a privileged family that appreciated and encouraged writing. In some ways, she followed societal norms. She married her husband, Leonard Woolf, in 1912, and authored novels including *Mrs. Dalloway* and *To the Lighthouse*.

In other ways, though, she *broke* societal norms. She never had children. She wrote feminist works like *A Room of One's Own* and *Three Guineas*. And she questioned the systems that had held women back from time immemorial, and still held women back to that day. (Women were only recently granted the right to vote in England when Woolf wrote *A Room of One's Own*.)

One thing I notice in Woolf's writing is a certain lack of humility. Frankly, it's refreshing! Studying history as much as I do, it can be *painful* to read anything written by women before the second half of the 20th century. The diffident tone, the qualifying language, the self-effacing phrasing — it had a purpose, which was to keep these women writers safer from the righteous anger of men who believed women shouldn't dare express themselves — but as a 21st century woman, it's hard to swallow.

To read Woolf's work is to witness a woman *pushing back.*

I think we could all stand to push back a little more.

Where is a societal norm keeping you from using your voice?

Where can you push back, even a little bit, for the sake of your work in the world?

For me, the answer was first in my career choice. When I was pregnant with my first child, my parents were horrified when I told them Jeremy was going to care for our new daughter while I went back to work in my corporate job and continued to freelance as a writer on the side. Never mind that I was *working from home* in that corporate job, or that both my corporate job and writing gigs paid significantly more than Jeremy was making at his job. I knew that quitting my job to raise children wasn't the right thing for my family at that time — and I knew it would make it impossible for me to keep writing.

    I'm happy to say my parents got over it rather quickly. Especially once they saw how amazing Jeremy is with a baby. But still, it felt like a huge leap for me, to say *I'm going to do this differently*. I couldn't imagine a life where I wasn't writing, and I couldn't write with a baby on my lap. (Some women can. I can't.) I used my voice to state my desire for something outside the norm, and I continued to use my voice in my writing. It was hard … and I'm so glad I did it.

Jane Goodall: Take Your Time

In 1960, at anthropologist Louis Leaky's prompting, Jane Goodall set out for Tanzania, Africa, to study chimpanzees in their natural habitat. Chimps' sensitivity to human presence had long been a challenge to scientists wishing to study them, but Leakey believed Goodall had something that would help her overcome that challenge and succeed where others failed: *patience*.

When her first attempts to get close to a wild group of chimpanzees failed, Goodall discovered that it was going to take even more time and patience for the chimps to endure her presence than she first anticipated.

She needed the chimps to not fear her, and to act naturally while she observed them so she could witness their normal behavior in the wild — and rushing the process would have the opposite effect.

Finding a new group of chimps to study, Goodall took a slow-and-steady approach to observing them. She went out every morning at the exact same time and sat quietly in the exact same place near their feeding area. Eventually the chimps got used to her, and she was able to move closer to them, bit by bit. Within a year, the group of chimps allowed her within 30 feet of their feeding area. Within two years, they were approaching *her*.

Goodall used what she learned from her time with the chimps to educate the scientific community and eventually the general public, and challenge long-held beliefs about chimps' behaviors, diet, capabilities, communication, and ultimately the differences between primates and humans. Through documentaries, speaking, articles and books, Goodall shared her work with the world.

What strikes me about Goodall's story is that she *took her time*. And I don't just mean she had patience with the wild chimps. I mean she TOOK the time she needed. She went to the place where she could do her work best and do her best work — and she didn't let anyone or anything rush her in or out of that place.

The first time I read *Llama Llama Red Pajama* to one of my daughters, I was horrified. It was — *is* — a popular children's book about a young llama who has a meltdown when his mother gets sidetracked by household tasks when she's supposed to be getting him a glass of water. I was horrified for the little llama, who trusted his mother to keep her word and then worried when she didn't. And I was horrified for the mama llama that she had so much to do that she got distracted from the small but important promise she made to her child.

What horrified me most, however, was that this story captured perfectly the constant demands we are subject to by everyone and everything in our lives: our loved ones, the phone ringing, the dirty dishes in the sink. It's a herculean task to keep up with it all ... but to take time away to do our work in the world? Impossible.

Or is it?

It feels like a lot to ask of our loved ones and our everyday lives to let us take a step away to do something that moves us toward our greater purpose. I think the price of *not* asking is greater, though.

One day a week where your partner takes care of the kids. Two long weekends a year to go on a retreat. An hour a day to call your own. A week on location. *These are not big asks.* It may feel huge, and it may feel like you're inconveniencing everyone to the point of baby llama meltdown — but in the grand scheme, taking a bit of time for your work is *not* a big ask. Your children won't forget who you are. Your spouse won't run off with someone else. Your colleagues can cover your workload. Your clients can plan around your absence. Jane Goodall took years — you can take a weekend.

The first time I went to a writers conference after I started having children, I admit, I felt like a terrible wife and mother. My poor husband was going to have to wake up with the baby *three whole days in a row*. My poor daughter was going to have separation anxiety, *I just knew it*. My clients were going to be furious that I wasn't there to complete their projects *immediately*. You know what *actually* happened? Everyone was fine. My family missed me, and I missed them — but everyone was okay. My clients didn't send out hunting parties. And I came home renewed, inspired, and with thousands of fresh words written in my work-in-progress. I was probably a much better human to be around the week after I came home!

Take the time you need. It might be hard the first time you do it. It might be hard the first few times. Do it anyway. Your spirit, your creative work, and even your loved ones will thank you for it.

Margaret Thatcher: Get Help — Unashamedly

When Margaret Thatcher went into the hospital to have her baby, she ended up with two surprises. The first was that she was unexpectedly delivering twins. The second was that while she was elated at being a mother, she was absolutely sure she still wanted a career too. In her own words, from *Margaret Thatcher: The Autobiography*:

> *"Indeed, I needed a career because, quite simply, that was the sort of person I was. And not just any career. I wanted one which would keep me mentally active and prepare me for the political future for which I believed I was well suited."*

There was no doubt in her mind that she wanted to continue to pursue her career in law and politics — and she knew it was going to take good time management and a great deal of in-home help to achieve it now with *two* children. Before she even left the hospital, she had sent for the application for the Bar finals — and by the time she was home and settled in with the twins, she had already arranged for a full-time nanny.

Thatcher is very matter-of-fact about this in her autobiography. Her career was important to her, so she hired someone to help her with the children during the week. On the weekends, she took over with the children and they had quality family time. When she became a member of parliament, she was often home after the kids were asleep at night — so to make sure she had time with her family, she insisted that everyone have breakfast together every morning.

This all sounds very reasonable ... and yet as I was reading Thatcher's story, I had to keep reminding myself that this was in England in the early 1950s. This wasn't reasonable then — it was blasphemy. And while Thatcher didn't appear to have any shame about pursuing a career and leaving her children in the hands of a nanny during workdays, people tried to shame her nonetheless.

She remarks in her book that it was actually *women* who were most vicious about judging her.

Let's be honest. That still happens way, way too much. We women judge each other so harshly. It's hard enough to make these choices in life — choices men have never had to make.

Instead of judging each other, let's support each other. And when someone tries to make us feel guilty for our life choices, let's remember that shame has no place in the pursuit of our dreams. Shame has no place on the canvas, the blank page, the podium or the field. Your work matters. What other people think about it *doesn't*.

So the challenge to you here is twofold: First, ask for the help you need. Second, do it without shame.

It took me years to convince Jeremy to let me hire a cleaning service to come to our house once a month. *Years.* He was a stay-at-home dad and I worked from home, and it felt weird to him that we would hire someone to come in and clean our house *when we were both there.* Yet fight after fight, we were lashing out at each other over the same stupid things that neither of us could seem to get a handle on in our day-to-day life together. Jeremy couldn't seem to manage to wipe the kitchen counters. I was averse to washing dishes at the end of a long workday, and neither of us did toilets. Instead of spending our weekends enjoying each other's company, we were bickering while we used what little remaining energy we had to tackle the messes of the week.

I knew a monthly deep-cleaning service was the perfect solution to this particular marital woe. Jeremy took some convincing.

Sure enough, when we finally did it, it was a marriage miracle. Our constant arguments stopped. Besides the fact that things were finally being taken care of — by people who did a WAY better job than we could do — I was so delighted by my sparkling clean house that it stopped bothering me when things started to get messier than I like as the sparkle wore off between cleanings.

Am I proud that years later, we *still* can't seem to keep a clean house when we're both home a lot? No. But I am proud that I took action and got help.

That help freed up mental space for me that I was then able to direct toward growing my business and doing my writing. Instead of scrubbing sinks when my kids are napping on the weekend, I'm writing this book.

It's a sacrifice, for sure. We had to give up other things to have the money to pay for a cleaning service. But it was one of the best investments I've made in my marriage, my sanity, and my work in this world. So I have zero shame about hiring professional help. I just wish more women felt the same.

This is a conversation I've had with so many women over the years. They think hiring help makes them *less than* somehow. Or they think it's too expensive, so it's too much of a luxury. Or — and this one's insidious — they think their partner just needs to step up and do more, and paying for help is letting them off the hook.

Here's the stark-naked truth: None of us are alone in this world. We all operate with help every day. From the mailman who delivers your Amazon packages and junk mail, to your child's teacher, to your creative writing group. We do very little *truly alone* in this world. We have a lot of help. Many of us don't color our own hair or do our own nails, but for some reason we feel like hiring help with the housework is ridiculous.

So why is there this cloud of shame over paying for more help when we need to and can afford it?

Up until the middle of the 20th century, while women had less help from their male partners in raising children and caring for the home, they actually had *more* help in other ways. Neighbors and communities offered help. Women helped each other. Nannies and housekeepers were staples in many middle-class homes as well. There was an understanding that a woman couldn't do it all by herself.

Now, for some strange reason, we expect to not only raise our children, take care of the house and tend to our relationships without help, but we're expected to do it while holding down a full-time job and baking gluten-free cookies for the school raffle.

That's insane.

Can you think of a single woman in history who did a great work in this world without *some* kind of help in her life? Even those rare birds you hear about who produced their work while caring for children full time, they're likely doing much of their work while their kids are in school being cared for by *paid teachers and administrators*.

(For the record, Stephenie Meyer, author of the Twilight series, apparently did her work with a child on her lap. She's the only example I've ever come across. So clearly it's possible ... but exceedingly rare.)

There is no shame in asking for help. Nor is there any shame in *expecting* help. We were not meant to navigate this world alone.

Is there an area of your life that you could ask for help with, or hire help for, that would free you to pursue your calling?

Frida Kahlo: Time Isn't Always What You Imagine It Will Be — Use It Anyway

If anyone deserved an easier life, it was artist Frida Kahlo. She contracted polio at the age of six, which kept her bedridden for nine months and resulted in permanent damage to her right leg and foot. She walked with a limp for the rest of her life. Even after she recovered from the disease, she was rejected and bullied by the other children in the neighborhood.

It was in those painful early years of her life that she began sketching. Some might even say that her early struggles are what spurred her to create and eventually become one of the most beloved artists of the 20th century.

Remarkable art birthed from great challenge — it's a powerful story. But this wasn't the only challenge Kahlo faced in her life, and those sketches weren't her only artistic contribution.

In 1925, around the age of 18, she was traveling home from school on a bus when there was a terrible accident. A streetcar smashed into the side of the bus, dragging it down the road. Many of the passengers died — and Kahlo was impaled by an iron handrail. Her spine, right leg, pelvic bone, and collarbone were broken, her shoulder dislocated, and the handrail punctured her abdomen and uterus.

Once again, Kahlo was bedridden for months.

Though she tried to continue her schoolwork during her lengthy and lonely convalescence, she was forced to drop out of school. It was at that time she took up painting to fill her time. She painted some of her first self-portraits on a special lap easel in bed, using an overhead mirror to see herself while she was lying down.

Over her lifetime, she had more than 30 surgeries and was never able to have children. Through her physical, mental and emotional pain, she continued to paint. It seems she painted from bed as often as she painted in a studio — and this is what inspires me most about Frida Kahlo.

I'm the first to use illness or stress as an excuse not to write. Not feeling 100% is a good reason to rest and recuperate instead of pushing myself. And while rest is incredibly important to our health and wellbeing, it can also be ... *addictive*. Once you lose momentum, it can be hard to get motivated to get moving again. This applies to making art as much as it applies to anything — physical exercise, organizing a social movement, meditating ...

Lethargy begets lethargy.

There are certainly situations where being down and out physically prevents you from doing your work in the world. But what if, when we were on the road to recovery, we stayed vigilant in our quest for time of our own?

This time wouldn't be free and clear, no. It's not *ideal* time in any way, shape or form. But just because this time isn't what you imagined it should be doesn't make it any less valuable.

And really, when is time of our own ever perfect?

What if, while you were in bed recovering from a cold, you turned off the soap operas for five minutes and scribbled down some ideas for your next network group meetup? What if in that half hour you were waiting for your child to get out of karate practice, you jotted down a few song lyrics? What if while the water was boiling for dinner, you grabbed a water brush and did a quick watercolor painting in your travel notebook? What if, while you were unable to walk after knee surgery, you knitted a few rows of that scarf you meant to finish last Christmas, or read a book by that author you admire?

What if you used just *some* of that deeply imperfect time to nurture your calling?

Emily Dickinson: Shut Out the World Sometimes

Emily Dickinson is as known for her reclusiveness as she is for her poetry. In fact, many would hold her up as a vivid example of how creativity flourishes with focus.

While she did produce much of her work in the years she was sequestered in the Dickinson family home known as the Homestead, the reality was *she wasn't alone.* Nor was she free from the responsibilities of caring for others. In fact, Emily Dickinson and her sister Lavinia were the primary caretakers of their chronically ill mother until she passed away in 1882 — a mere four years before Emily herself died of kidney disease.

For most of Dickinson's life, she lived with and cared for family.

She did, however, shut out the world at large in her later years. No one is quite sure why. Theories include agoraphobia and depression. It's possible, though, that caring for her mother was more than enough for her to handle. It's possible that she was reclusive because she chose to spend what little energy she had left on her work in the world — her poetry, a lavish garden and an extensive herbarium including 424 pressed flower specimens.

Dickinson took shutting out the world to an extreme, no doubt. But I still think there's something we can take away from her story. Caring for a sick family member is an exhausting, deeply emotional, full-time job — and Dickinson was still able to find enough focus to produce nearly 1,800 poems.

We can learn to tune out so we can tune *in*.

I've worked from home since 2007. Since before I was married, and before I had kids. I thought I was practiced at tuning out the sounds of my family and focusing on my client work during the workdays … until I bought a really good pair of headphones in 2019.

I'd been eyeing a pair of Bose noise-canceling headphones for years. Several of my copywriting peers had gushed to me about how much they loved theirs, and couldn't imagine working without them. I just didn't see the point in spending that much money when I could crank up a white noise track on a music streaming service when I needed to drown out distractions.

It wasn't until a client sent me an Amazon gift card as a thank-you gift that I finally caved. With that gift card, I bought the Bose headphones — not the really high-end ones, but a middle-of-the road, wired model.

The moment I put them over my ears and flipped the noise-cancelation switch, *I got it*. I completely understood my fellow copywriters' obsession. I wasn't just drowning out the little noises all around me ... *the world went quiet.* It was like I was transported somewhere else, somewhere more peaceful.

To this day, I wear those headphones every single day when I'm writing — for both client work and my own work. I wear them at home and I wear them at the executive suite I now rent downtown. There's something about shutting out the world even in this small way that makes my writing flow more easily.

In fact, wearing those headphones is one of the few ways I'm able to get into the "flow state." (Defined by psychologist Mihály Csíkszentmihályi in 1975, *flow state* is when you are fully immersed in what you are doing, you feel energized and fully focused, and time flies by.)

Getting into the flow state becomes incredibly challenging when you're doing your creative, world-changing work in a place where other people are making a racket. Having kids makes it feel almost impossible. It's not enough to tune out the noise or find a babysitter so you can go off to a quiet place alone. A mother's mind is still distracted because part of her attention is *always* on her children. Even when they're not with her.

Space of our own and time of our own are great starts — but we need more in order to heed our life calling. We need to be able to focus. *Without worry or guilt.*

As I write this, I hear Jeremy and my children downstairs. Their voices are happy. They seem to be playing together. I feel my attention drawn to them, as hard as I'm trying to focus on writing this. When I pay attention, there are so many other noises — birds chirping, soft music playing, cars in the distance — and my attention isn't drawn to them as it is to my children.

This may be controversial, and many mothers may disagree with me, but I don't believe this is entirely biological. I believe there is a heavy cultural component. Today we are taught that our children must be the center of our lives or we're bad mothers. We're told there are dangers lurking around every corner, and we must always be hyperalert to protect our babes. And while yes, in some ways there are more or new threats than in generations before, no matter how safe our children are in the moment, our attention is on them. This is a killer of creative flow, and why so many mothers, especially of young children, struggle in their creative pursuits.

Sometimes, to do our work in the world, we have to shut *out* the world for a little while. Yes, it's hard, especially if you have children (or aging parents, I would assume, though I can't speak directly to that … yet). But is there a small way you can do this right now? Can you put on a pair of headphones? Can you send your family out for ice cream without you? Can you get away to a quiet place for a few hours, or a few days?

Lost and Found

CHAPTER 7

My Story

I feel like I've trudged a million miles uphill to get where I am today — and I'm nowhere near the end of my journey. My work in this world is writing (and dabbling in art a bit), and while I've done a pretty good job at keeping a general focus on that in my career, I've certainly gone off track in many ways. Still, I always make my way back here, to the page. There have been seasons where long stretches of time have passed between good, purposeful writing sessions — but I always find my way back.

Many women over the years have told me that my story inspired them and gave them the confidence they needed to keep pursuing their calling. I don't think I'm any kind of expert, but I will admit that my story is an unusual one, and I think there are lessons to be learned from it.

My prayer as you read this is that you can take the lessons from this story and never experience the heartbreaks.

CHAPTER 8

The Time I Lost and the Time I Gained

Like many women, I'm sure, I had romantic ideas about having children. I imagined getting pregnant as soon as we decided we were ready, being bathed in love from the moment I saw the positive pregnancy test, being doted on by my husband through my pregnancy, having one of those it-was-so-easy birth stories that makes other women jealous, and being so totally enamored with my child that painful nursing and inevitable sleep deprivation would feel like no big deal. I imagined writing while my baby napped.

The reality was so much different.

Jeremy and I struggled to conceive our first child. When we finally had our first little girl, Scarlett Rose, I was 30 years old and climbing the ranks in a corporate job while freelancing as a copywriter after hours. The struggle to conceive had put a huge strain on our marriage, and we had moved near Boulder, Colorado, away from all our friends and family to focus on repairing the damage. Jeremy had left his job when we moved, and he hadn't been able to find a new job in our new location. I, on the other hand, was working remotely and making pretty decent money. When Scarlett was born, it made sense for Jeremy to stop searching for a job and instead take on the role of stay-at-home dad.

It was the perfect solution for so many reasons. Besides the job situation, our personalities were well-suited to these non-traditional roles.

Jeremy is known in our extended family as "the baby whisperer" — kids love him, and he is amazing with them. Plus, he has never needed the social interaction that I have needed to be mentally and emotionally healthy. He was, and is to this day, perfectly happy at home.

I, on the other hand, am your typical Type A. I need structure in my day and a goal to work toward. I am ambitious and I love a good challenge. I'm competitive and confident, and I knew that I could do more than work a corporate job the rest of my life. I knew that my side gig as a copywriter could grow into something bigger someday if I just set my mind to it. I loved our daughter with all my heart — but I was a better mother and a better human being if I had a job.

Scarlett had colic. If you're a parent reading this, you probably just got shivers down your spine because you know just how hard it is on *everyone*. If you're not a parent, let me explain it to you this way: Colic is when your infant cries non-stop for no reason and there's nothing you can do to make them stop. There are a million theories about what causes colic (reflux, an immature nervous system, a milk allergy ... the list is long and very broad), and a million recommendations for what to do about it (swaddle the baby tight, keep her head at an angle while she sleeps, feed her soy formula ...). Most of the time, though, colic isn't solvable — it's a waiting game. Babies usually outgrow it sometime between month 9-12. In the meantime, you have a baby that *won't stop crying no matter what you do*.

By the time I was done with work for the day, my husband needed a break from the screaming baby. And I didn't blame him one bit. So for the first 9 months of Scarlett's life, by the time she went to bed at night, I had maybe two hours before it was time for *me* to go to bed. And thanks to the marriage counseling we had gone through by that point (marriage counseling is a lifesaver — I firmly believe *every* married couple should do it!), Jeremy and I knew that at least some of that time needed to be bonding time for *us* in order to keep our marriage healthy.

Weekends? When I wasn't working on freelance projects, I was taking care of Scarlett. Besides my desire to give Jeremy a break from his full-time-dad duties, that was some of the only time I had with her.

My time hadn't just shrunk … it had disappeared entirely.

When Scarlett turned one, the colic was done with and she was starting to sleep through the night more often than not. Here and there, I started squeezing in an hour of painting before I went to bed at night. It wasn't enough to completely "fill my cup," as the self-care gurus say, but it felt good. It was *something* creative.

This went on for another seven months or so. After Scarlett went to bed, I'd have some time with my husband, and then I'd go do something creative or self-care-focused before bed. I got back to my old habit of reading before bed, too, which really added to the feeling of finally having a bit of "me time" again.

On February 23, 2012, it all came crashing down. I found Scarlett dead in her crib.

This book isn't a memoir. It's not a horror story, either. I won't go into detail about the events of that day or the year that followed. I will tell you, though, that they never found a cause. Scarlett's pediatrician, who was as devastated as anyone, told us the term for it is "SUDC" — sudden unexpected death of a child. It's the term they use for a SIDS-like death when the child is over 12 months old. Her body just ... stopped. It stopped for no reason. It's a mystery that will never be solved, and that I've had to grow to live with.

The emotional tornado that followed would have shaken any marriage, but I'm happy to tell you that Jeremy and I beat the odds. We held onto each other and we made it through together.

After the funeral, I threw myself into my work. Like a madwoman, I focused on growing my fledgling copywriting business with the goal of leaving my corporate job and becoming fully self-employed.

It was a year before I could pick up a paintbrush again. It was even longer before I felt like I could write anything besides client marketing projects and personal blog posts. Photography, writing for hiking guidebooks, knitting ... the things I once loved didn't seem to matter anymore. And I certainly couldn't afford the time to do them. Not when I had a business to grow. Especially not when we started down the road to IVF (in-vitro fertilization).

In the years after Scarlett passed, we wanted to have more children. And though both Jeremy and I had passed all the medical tests with flying colors, we were unable to conceive again. Most medical professionals thought stress was the culprit. Even if it was, how do you not feel stressed after you lose your first and only baby?

IVF was brutal. Whatever time and energy I had left in my life, it was taken up by precisely-timed injections, naps driven by hormone rollercoasters, and endless, *endless* doctor appointments.

In the fall of 2014, I was finally pregnant again.

Shortly after we got the positive pregnancy test, the company I was working for decided they were moving all remote employees back to the office. The nearest office to where we lived was an hour away. I knew the time had come to leave my corporate job.

Pregnant with my second child and absolutely terrified, I told my manager that the next time she had to lay off an employee (it was a large tech company — layoffs happened with stunning regularity), I was raising my hand. Still, I was a little surprised that the layoff came within weeks. I scrambled to prepare for it.

I'm proud to say that before my second daughter, Autumn, was born, I grew my little freelance copywriting business into something that supported our family.

When Autumn was born, two weeks early and much smaller than anyone anticipated, colic hell started all over again. This time we were not only suffering from the constant crying, we were also terrified every minute of every day that she would die like her sister did. We bought all the latest monitoring devices on the market — a video monitor, a breathing monitor, and eventually, when it was available, a smart sock that monitored Autumn's pulse and oxygen levels while she slept.

Time for anything other than breathing, eating, and the occasional shower seemed like a pipe dream. And energy for anything other than the work I had to do to earn a living? Long gone.

Autumn didn't sleep through the night until she was two years old. She never wanted to be by herself — asleep or awake. Maybe our fear had seeped into her bones. I don't know.

We wanted more children. We wanted Autumn to have at least one sibling — more if possible. When I found out I was pregnant again at the end of 2016, we were over the moon! We had conceived without medical intervention. It was a miracle.

In January of 2017, I miscarried. It felt like a cosmic joke. Not only had I lost my first baby, now I was losing a second.

The devastating loss, combined with the growing acceptance that Autumn may never have any siblings, drove us to make another move. We moved back down to Colorado Springs so Autumn could grow up near most of her cousins.

When we had been settled into our new home in Colorado Springs for a year or so, I suddenly realized that I was okay having only one child. I didn't want to do IVF again. And Autumn is an *amazing* kid. We were so blessed! We were a family of three, and I was happy with that. For the first time since Scarlett was born, I finally started looking *forward* again — thinking about traveling, getting a social life, and taking up new hobbies.

Then I found out I was pregnant again. Cosmic joke, take four.

Cassandra was a surprise in every possible way. My body did not take kindly to being pregnant for the fourth time at almost 40 years old. It was a miserable nine months. Eight days after she was born, her smart sock sounded a low-oxygen alarm in the middle of the night, and we rushed her to the hospital. Her oxygen levels were indeed low, but it turns out this is a relatively normal thing that happens with babies born at high altitude. Still, after losing Scarlett, we were terrified — and the doctors were extra cautious. The hospital sent Cassie home on supplemental oxygen and told us she'd be fine in a few months.

Picture trying to nurse a baby with oxygen tubes strapped to her face, connected to oxygen cords connected to highly flammable oxygen tanks. Moving her from room to room took an army. Meanwhile, we were trying to keep almost-four-year-old Autumn from tripping over the cords, the tanks, and all the other gear that came with a newborn on supplemental oxygen.

For the three months that Cassie was on oxygen, we didn't leave the house.

Time for doing my creative work? Forget it.

Cassie came with two unexpected blessings, though. First, she did *not* have colic. Second, she was a champion sleeper.

When she was four months old, off of supplemental oxygen, and sleeping through the night (yes, at four months old — miracles do happen!), I finally started getting full nights of sleep again. I really thought that after a few months of good sleep, I'd get my energy back for doing my creative work.

But trauma doesn't let you off that easy.

Whether it was underlying fear from losing Scarlett, psychological damage from having two babies with colic before this, or just normal parental anxiety, full nights of sleep did not equal energy for anything other than caring for my family and running my business. And once again, when I wasn't working, I was with my kids. I felt like I had no time or motivation for *anything*.

Cassie was more than a year old when I started coming out of that haze. I finally started taking time out of my workday for ME — going to the gym, having lunch with a friend, taking a break to go for a walk in the middle of the day. I finally stopped feeling guilty for asking Jeremy if he would watch the kids on the weekend so I could attend a class or a lecture.

At age 40, I started emerging from what felt like a long sleep. Until one day I woke up and realized that 10 years had gone by.

I had spent *10 years* trying to get pregnant, being pregnant, and having babies. I had spent *10 years* growing my family and my business — and *my* work in the world, *my* creative pursuits hadn't just been put on hold, they had been stuffed in a suitcase and thrown in a river.

I was 40 years old with a thriving business and two young kids, I was exhausted ... *and I wanted more than that.*

I had learned two important lessons in those 10 years. The first was that there is only so much pressure I can put on myself before my rubber bands start snapping, the bits flying at those I love. And second is that time is malleable.

Death Ground

In his *33 Strategies of War*, Robert Greene writes about the concept of "death ground." In the context of war, it means putting your army in a position where the only way to get out alive is to win. Desperation gives humans the will to fight.

As a big fan of deadlines as motivators, I embrace this idea wholeheartedly ... and yet I also think it can also be destructive to the work we're doing in the world. Often we wait to be put on death ground before we take action — we procrastinate until it's do-or-die. This sucks the life out of us *and* our work.

Death ground is too much pressure, the rubber bands start stretching and straining, and snap with the slightest tug. I experienced this firsthand when I wrote a book in my third trimester while I was pregnant with Autumn.

I was in agony. I'd gone through months of painful medical treatments in order to conceive Autumn with my husband.

I was terrified every day that I would lose her like I lost her sister before her. My body was rebelling — whether it was all the extra hormones I had been dosed with (and was still being dosed with to make sure my body stayed in "optimal" condition to carry a baby), or it was simply my "advanced maternal age" (I laughed at this designation at 35), my body was coming apart at the seams. Before my belly even began to bulge, my hip joints felt like they were ripping apart, my knees felt arthritic, I was having heart palpitations and reflux every night, and I was getting migraines weekly.

If ever there were a season to pause my work in the world, this would be it.

But while this longed-for child was triggering my body to go haywire, I also knew what was coming at the end of it. I'd been here before. At that time, since Scarlett had passed away years before, we were childless. We had all the time in the world to do what we wanted to do. But unlike most couples without children, we knew from experience what we were in for once this new baby arrived. What *I* was in for. Sleep deprivation. Round-the-clock feeding and diaper changing. *Colic*, if she were anything like her sister. No matter how much pain I was in, I knew this would be my last chance for a long while to do any meaningful projects.

I knew when this baby came, *my* life — my time — would be paused indefinitely.

My new baby's birth was my death ground.

This is the thing about newborns. You disappear into them. And there's no telling how long it'll be until you reemerge. Maybe you'll reemerge when the baby starts sleeping through the night. Maybe you'll *never* fully reemerge. A child in my extended family has severe genetic disorders, and his parents have vanished into that beautiful boy's orbit for almost 11 years now.

I felt it so strongly when I was pregnant with Autumn — if I didn't write a book now, I might never do it. And if I never wrote another book ... what if I resented my daughter for it? I couldn't risk it. I knew no matter how hard it was, I had to finish writing this book I had been planning to write.

I was *driven*. I hired a writing coach to give me an accountability boost, planned out the writing, and got to work ... with 12 weeks to go before the baby was due.

Looking back, I wonder if I was trying to prove something to myself.

Nonetheless, I wrote the book in 8 weeks. I hustled my rear off, spending every extra minute I had writing, editing, and designing. Jeremy and I hardly had any time together in the final stretch of that pregnancy.

By the end, I *hated* that book. I put it up for sale on my consulting website two weeks before Autumn was born, and I never even marketed it.

Honestly, it wasn't a great book. I wasn't proud of it at all. I had rushed through the work and thrown it out into the world like a hot potato instead of treating it like a cherished piece of work that I wanted people to read.

I got it done. But it didn't feel good. And it cost me precious time with my husband during the last weeks we would ever be childless again.

Writing that book wasn't a total waste of time, however. It served an important purpose. When I had Autumn (and as I had feared, she had that dreaded colic), and I was terrified every moment that she slept, and utterly entranced every moment she was awake (even though she was screaming in my face most of that time), the season of pause was so much easier to bear. I'd gotten that work out of me, and now I could enjoy this little bit of "rest." (Ha! Rest. Any mother reading this knows that the only rest in the newborn season is rest from pushing yourself to do anything beyond brushing your teeth and showering once in a while.)

Still, I'll always wonder if that book would have had a bigger, better impact in this world if I hadn't waited until I was on death ground to write it.

Time Bending

At 40 years old, I knew I had to make a decision. I could either embrace the seed God had planted in my heart to be an author — or I could finally let it go. I had this deep need in me to make a decision one way or the other.

Perhaps this was because of everything that 40 represented to me — the beginning of middle age, the end of my childbearing years, the point at which retirement planning becomes serious.

Or perhaps it was because I was doing a lot of math. I had my last baby at 39 — so I'd be 57 at her high school graduation, and likely retirement age when she got married and started having kids. *What did that look like?* I couldn't imagine it. I literally had acquaintances my exact age *who were grandparents.*

And while I was thinking about these things, I was also realizing that my young-and-healthy years were rushing by at an astonishing pace. I didn't feel like 40 was old by any stretch of the imagination, and all of my grandparents had lived to ripe old ages — but I'd experienced enough death in my life (my little brother, most recently) to know that tomorrow is not guaranteed.

So I did what any reasonable Gen-Xer would do in a semi-midlife-crisis: I started experimenting with my routines and habits, then I hired a career coach. I figured something in that mix would give me the answer that I needed.

I have been an obsessive time-tracker for years. Yes, I'm self-employed, and no, I don't charge an hourly rate — but for my own knowledge, and to help me keep tabs on how long projects are taking me so I can give more accurate quotes for future projects, I use the Toggl app during my workday to track how I'm spending my time. So my workday routines and habits, at least, were relatively easy to experiment with.

I tried meditating when I first got to my office in the morning. I tried reading a book before I answered any emails. I tried journaling as my computer booted up. What

I learned was that I could do something for myself in the first hour or two of the day and no one got upset about it. Clients weren't pounding down my virtual door. There were no nasty emails waiting in my inbox. Work waited.

Work waited.

I started to wonder what else could wait.

Because Autumn was such a terrible sleeper, I had trained myself to get as much sleep as I could because I expected to be awakened at any moment. So even though after age two, she slept through the night with few problems, and even though Cassie was a champion sleeper from four months onward, I was still going to bed at 9 p.m. to make *sure* I could get my eight hours. I remembered something, though, at age 40: *I used to be a night owl.* What if I still was, really?

I decided I was going to stay up late each night for one week and write before I went to bed. Jeremy and I put the kids to bed around 7, we had some "couple time" until around 9, and then I headed up to the bedroom with my laptop. I admit, I was nervous. I had been so sleep-deprived for so many years, and I was finally starting to feel normal (whatever that is when you're a parent), what if this set me back? What if I was a zombie the next day? Or if not the next day, in a few days once the late nights caught up with me?

The result was better than I could have hoped for. Not only was I able to write more easily at night, but the house was quiet and I could really focus. For years I had this strange insomnia where I would wake 30 minutes after I went to sleep, though I was normally able to get right back to sleep — and now I had zero insomnia. I was able to wake in the morning at my usual time with no more trouble, too. I started by going to bed at 11, but within a week I was up to 11:30.

Looking at my routines and habits was like taking a magnifying glass to how I was spending every minute of my day. Working with a career coach, on the other hand was like pulling out a telescope to explore the expanse of my entire life.

When I hired Kori, I felt lost. I was burned out on my copywriting career. I was tired of the hustle to get new projects, tired of chasing overdue invoices, and tired of going back to work after the kids went to bed to stay ahead of an ever-growing task list.

I was also feeling trapped in the online marketing bubble. Copywriting falls firmly under the umbrella of marketing, and the marketing industry has gotten sick. It was all big promises and little lies, big paydays and little payouts, big growth and little ethics. Open communication and trust are the values I've built my career on, and I felt totally misaligned with my industry. I also felt like I was in an echo chamber. I decided that a career coach completely outside my industry, who knew no one in my virtual business circles, might help me to see past my own nose.

Admittedly, I thought she might be able to help me identify a career path that had nothing to do with writing. I had convinced myself that copywriting would kill me, and being an author (my lifelong dream) would make me go broke.

The work was hard. The first several weeks involved a lot of introspection, a lot of going back to my childhood and early adulthood, exploring who I was, and discovering what remained — and what didn't. On the one hand, I felt like I had strayed so far from my core self, and on the other hand I was surprised that so much childhood joy still remained inside me. I was still enamored with nature, still endlessly curious about how the world works, and still a *writer*.

As I examined my current life against the values I identified through the coaching process, I realized that I wasn't as far off track as I thought I was. I was still pretty well aligned with what matters to me. And copywriting, though still a marketing function, *was still writing*. It's a different way of using words, and its purpose is unique (the purpose of copywriting, ultimately, is to sell something), but as I honed that skill to a fine point, and grew my reputation along with my business, it sharpened my skills in other areas as well. Namely, the skills required to write and market books.

It turns out, though I'd gone astray from my childhood dream of being an author, and I was preparing to let that dream go once and for all, I had positioned myself to be one.

It was like the clouds parted and the angels started chanting melodically, "Write, write write!" That's when I realized that writing wasn't just something I liked to do and was good at. It was bigger than that. It was my work in the world. It was my calling. It was the seed God had planted, and I somehow managed to nurture all these years without even realizing it.

As I told Kori about how I had fiddled with my morning and nighttime routines to try to fit in more writing, reading and research, and how I didn't think I'd ever be able to make a living as an author with the way the publishing industry works these days, I stepped outside my body. I listened to myself speak, and something at the back of my mind whispered, *This is what you've been telling other women for years. The work they feel moved to do in this world is important. It doesn't matter if they make a living at it. All that matters is that they take, make, or find time to do it. It's not just self care — it's soul care.*

I'm still working through what it means to pursue my writing outside the structure of my established and hard-won copywriting career. But it's now taking priority in my life.

It feels like my spirit has stepped back into my body.

CHAPTER 9

When Time Is Paused

There are seasons of life when time slows down or even comes to a complete stop. Moments that seize us, like an unexpected death; and long, languid seasons where our attention is fully, and rightly, on another human being.

Having a baby is such a season. As is caring for an ailing spouse or aging parent. Sometimes there is no one to help us, even if we are courageous enough to ask. Sometimes it *must* be us stepping out of *our* time and into someone else's.

It can feel like a great sacrifice. It can feel like a great honor. It can feel like it will never end ... or you may never *want* it to end.

I don't honestly know if men feel seasons this way. But I'm sure most women do. This is the way we move through the world, after all, in cycles, in seasons, in turns.

There are seasons in this life that will demand you push the pause button on your work. That's life, and it's valid. I hope there are ideas in this book that help you carve out the time you need in the thriving, comfortable, and unrestricted seasons — but if you're in a season right now that demands a pause, remember, *this is a book*. You can always come back to it later.

Embrace the pause when you must.

All I ask is that you truly *consider* your season. Sit with it. Roll it around between your fingertips and get a genuine feel for it. Is this a season of embracing a pause? Or are you making excuses for not doing your work in the world?

If the answer is embracing a pause, that's okay. *It's okay*. Your work will be there for you when you can press play again.

Conclusion

Mustangs in a World of Pretty Ponies

It's painful to think about what my grandmothers and the women before them went through. It's painful to think about how limited they were, how under their husbands' thumbs they were.

My grandmother who raised seven children was a very stoic woman. She was college educated yet never held a job. From what I've been told by family members who knew her better than I did, her priority was always my grandfather. My grandfather insisted on being the center of his family's universe, like some domineering male character out of *Mad Men*.

I remember my grandmother, who passed away several years ago now, as being kind enough. She was proper, and rigid in the routines of her days, and her smile never reached her eyes, but I knew she cared for me. As I grew into adulthood, though, I wondered if her smile was hiding something. I wondered if she had trained herself to smile, no matter the circumstances. As she aged and I matured, I found myself feeling sad for her. I wondered if she had dreams that were never realized. I wondered if there was more inside of her that never got expressed.

My grandfather left a small estate for my grandmother, and combined with her own modest family inheritance she was secure enough to stay in the house where she raised her seven children. She never wanted for necessities. She did crossword puzzles, taught exercise classes at the local senior center, and played hostess for a never-ending train of family visitors. She loved receiving letters, and she wrote lovely recollections of her family's history to those who asked for it. I wondered, was she a *writer* underneath it all?

Today my hope is that my children and my children's children never wonder these things about me. I hope the generations of women who come after me never dampen their own spirits or muffle their own voices. I hope their spirits sing loudly through their work in the world, whatever it may be.

Until my mother's generation — and probably later than that, if we're being honest — a woman's spirit was seen as a wild and dangerous thing. I agree it's wild — wildly beautiful like a herd of mustangs. And yes, a woman's spirit can even be dangerous to the status quo, to the systems that have kept us humbled and oppressed for millennia. We have more work to do in this world to make it a safe and welcoming place for women to step forward, but we've come so far. We can speak out and be heard more safely than any other time in history.

So let's let our spirits loose like those wild mustangs. Let's use our voices to spread love, create change, open minds, propagate beauty and make this world better for everyone in it. Now is not the time to make yourself small like those learned women of Renaissance Italy had to in order to be heard. Now is the time to express yourself with confidence. Don't go through life hiding your light inside you: Reveal it so we can all bask in its glow. Reveal it and light the way for generations to come.

Works Cited

Schulte, Brigid. (2019, July) *A woman's greatest enemy? A lack of time to herself.*
https://www.theguardian.com/commentisfree/2019/jul/21/woman-greatest-enemy-lack-of-time-themselves

Whyte, David. *The Three Marriages*. Brilliance Audio, 2009

Holiday, Ryan. *Stillness Is the Key*. Portfolio, 2019

Woolf, Virginia. *A Room of One's Own*. Penguin Books, London, 1945

Thatcher, Margaret. *Margaret Thatcher: The Autobiography*, Harper Perennial; Abridged, Combined edition (April 9, 2013)

Greene, Robert. *33 Strategies of War*. Penguin Group, New York, 2007

Acknowledgements

This book exists because Alexandra Franzen and Lindsey Smith taught me that tiny books can change the world. I thank them from the bottom of my heart for encouraging me to take action.

The biggest thanks, however, go to my family. To my husband for always believing in me. To my daughters for inspiring me every day. To my mother for showing me that this world holds endless possibilities. To my father for revealing the beauty of reaching higher. To my brother Drew for putting up with me. And finally, to my brother Chad, who never got the chance to read this book, and who would have been so proud of me for writing it.

About the Author

Jessica Mehring is a Colorado-based author, copywriter and entrepreneur. She believes that history and nature are our greatest teachers, yet she is also endlessly fascinated by technology and the human brain. She loves reading, walks in the woods, yoga, and creating and collecting art. She lives with her husband, two daughters, and one spoiled mutt — and her growing collection of books and office supplies are slowly taking over their house.

You can connect with Jessica at jessicamehring.com.

Women in Time and Space

www.ingramcontent.com/pod-product-compliance
Lightning Source LLC
Chambersburg PA
CBHW071400080526
44587CB00017B/3147